Earth

Mother

Magick

Ella C Moon

~*~ Dedication ~*~

This book is dedicated to all the earth lovers, the
shamans, and the planetary healers...

It is with our love and respect,
That we can heal her
Back into the greatness
She once was,
And because of us,
Will be again...

And to Bruno...

~*~ Book Blessing ~*~

May the songs
Sung by the winds,
Be whispered
Into the hearts
Of the Witches
Who stir the cauldrons
And cast the spells,
And may the magick
Flow from these pages
And heal the Earth.
Blessed be!

~*~ Table of Contents ~*~

Connection

Many people will say they feel a connection to nature, or a connection to the earth, but what is it they are actually connecting to?

There is a web of ley lines, or energy lines, that surround the earth. Many people have felt this energy grid, and not even realized that is what they were tapping into.

Connecting with the ley lines of the earth can be a wonderful experience, and can bring a tremendous amount of power to magickal workings, especially those workings involving earth magick.

Finding this web of energy is relatively easy, if you are near one of the ley lines, as they are easily felt when encountered. For those who aren't as sensitive to energy as others may be, these lines can be found by the use of dowsing rods. Copper rods work best when locating energy, versus wood when witching for water.

Once a ley line is located, connection is easy, as it automatically happens, naturally. Once the connection is made, it will be very obvious, as the energy will channel through you at a different vibration than your natural resonation.

This vibration can be felt throughout your entire being, due to the strength of the energy grid.

Many people who encounter ley line connection feel overwhelmed by the energy shift, and can even experience symptoms of illness. Usually, those affected so strongly, are very sensitive to energy, and know how to handle such encounters if they accidentally happen.

When purposely connecting to this energy grid, the energy can be quite a charge, and can be drawn up to use in many types of magick to strengthen and heal the earth.

This energy can also be used to empower magickal tools, talismans, bundles, crystals, and so much more!

What if you are not near a ley line? You can still connect. The ley lines are a massive grid, covering the planet like a blanket. No matter where you are, you are either near a ley line, or are within a boxed section of the grid. If you are within a section, you can draw up the connection from all around you.

It may not feel as strong, but the earth energy is the earth energy, no matter how the connection is made. The connection might not feel as powerful as it is standing directly on a ley line, but the power is still obtainable. Connection is the goal.

Once you recognize what the connection feels like, it will be easy to connect to going forward.

Walking in Nature

An easy way to connect is by taking a walk in nature. A walk in nature has more benefits than not. Walking is a wonderful form of exercise, which benefits everyone who is able to take a stroll in the woods.

Even those who have difficulty walking can enjoy being out in nature. Surrounding oneself with fresh air, sunshine, a gentle breeze, the smells and sounds of nature, can be very healing to the soul. Even if the exposure is short lived, the healing happens, naturally.

While out in nature, make a conscious effort to feel the earth connection. Feel the energy fill you, healing you, and giving you a power boost.

Meditating while out in nature is a wonderful experience that is highly recommended! The connection made while meditating is quite amazing, and very healing.

Grounding and Centering Energy

When working with any energy that is not your natural resonation, you can build up extra energy, which, if not released, can shift your natural vibration into overload, and can cause you to be jittery, clumsy, scattered, or even sick. This occurs often, and is easily fixed by handling the extra energy.

There are a couple of ways that this extra energy can be handled. One if the easiest ways to rid yourself of extra energy is to ground and center.

Grounding your energy is very important, and can be done discreetly, if need be. As you stand firm on the earth, feel the energy growing out of the souls of your feet, down through the earth, as if there are energy roots connecting you to the core of the earth.

As these energy roots grow, they strengthen your stance, grounding you firmly. Once well grounded, you can draw up any needed energy from the earth to center and balance your vibration. This act will be a noticeable shift in your personal energy, so there will be no question as to when it is complete. You will feel it.

When working directly with another energy source that is not the earth energy, as when working with the energy of another person or with some form of energy healing, a good method for grounding the extra energy is to stick your hands directly on the earth and allowing that energy to be absorbed into the earth energy.

When using this earth cleansing method, if the extra energy you are trying to remove is really heavy or sticky, it may be helpful to dig your hands down into the soil, or cleanse your hands in the soil using a washing motion, in which the soil will act as soap.

This cleansing method will aid in the stripping of the unwanted energy, and will recharge your hands after energy work.

Once the energy is stripped off of you, it is important to be sure you did not remove any of your personal energy that you will need for yourself in this process.

Another way to shake off extra energy is to wash it off in running water. This method is common when conducting a healing or direct energy work.

Some like to wash the energy off into a basin of water, usually adding crystals or herbs and flowers to the water to assist with cleansing of the energy.

When using this method, be sure to empty the basin onto the earth, so that extra energy can be absorbed and recycled into the earth energy.

Earth Mother Meditation

As mentioned earlier, meditation does wonders for the soul, and can assist in aligning body, mind, and spirit, which is crucial for those looking to obtain spiritual balance.

This basic meditation can be easily adapted to fit your needs, if you choose to do so.

It can be practiced privately, or in a group setting, and can be done in nature or indoors, all to your preference. This meditation will connect you to the spirit of the earth, known as Earth Mother.

Sit or lay in a comfortable position, and make sure you are in a safe place, not easily disturbed.

Start by closing your eyes and taking three deep breaths. As you breathe in, draw in golden light, allowing it to fill your entire being. As you exhale, breathe out grey, or dirty, light, making sure any pent up stress, anxiety, anger, or negativity is leaving within that grey light.

While your body is filled with golden light, allow it to seep into your muscles, relaxing them instantly. Allow it to penetrate your bones, organs, tissue, and blood. Feel the golden light filter through your whole body, relaxing you completely.

Once relaxed, visualize yourself in nature, and allow yourself to attune to the energies of nature that are all around you. Feel the sunshine on your skin, smell the sweet scents of nature blowing gently on you as the wind caresses you.

Visualize yourself walking down a shaded, but cleared path, leading into a thick wooded area. Follow the path without fear, know that you are completely safe and welcomed.

As this path leads you deeper into the woods, you see an animal approach you as if you were an old friend. Embrace this animal being, and ask it to join you on your journey. Allow this animal friend to guide you into a clearing, with one very large tree in the center.

Walk around this large tree, looking very closely at it, paying attention to detail. You will find a crack in the mighty bark. Slip your fingers inside the crack. As you do so, you will notice the crack grow so large; you can slip right into it with ease.

Slide yourself into the crack in the bark, and feel the energy of the tree pulsate around you. Allow the pulsing of the tree to match your heartbeat. This will bring you in alignment with the tree.

Once you align with the tree energy, feel the root system of the tree under your feet. Notice, as it begins to move and clear an opening for you to climb down into the soil beneath the mighty tree. As you climb down, you will see the ground open up a tunnel for you.

Allow yourself to enter the tunnel with ease. Follow the tunnel until it opens up into a cave. The walls of this cave are made of the most beautiful crystals you have ever seen. Feel the energy of these crystals penetrate through you, feel the tingling sensation they give with their strong vibration.

From the darkness of the cave, approaches a brilliant emerald green light. Allow this light to meet you in the crystal filled cavern. As the light gets closer, you can start to see the shape of a spirit take form. Feel the love from this spirit as she appears at your side, fully revealed.

This is the spirit of the Earth Mother. Embrace her, and share your love with her. You are in a safe place, protected, and surrounded by the purest love vibration.

Spend some time with the Earth Mother, tell her what you would like to share with her, and ask her any questions you may have. Listen to her stories as she shares her wisdom and insight with you.

When you are ready to part ways, offer your love and healing to her, as you say your goodbye to the Earth Mother. Allow her to fade back into the brilliant emerald green light as she drifts back into the darkness of the cave.

Once she is completely out of sight, start your journey back through the tunnel, up the roots of the mighty tree, and back out of the crack in the bark. You will notice your animal friend is waiting for you there, to guide you back out of the clearing and onto the path that awaits you.

As you walk back through the shady pathway, you will see the safe place you started from. Once you return to that spot, take three more deep breaths, and slowly open your eyes.

Be still for a moment, and remember your experience. If you can, document everything in detail into a meditation journal or book of shadows, so you don't forget any lessons or messages you received from the Earth Mother.

Open Heart to Earth Mother Ceremony

This ceremony will create a heart to heart connection between you and the Earth Mother. Once established, this heart to heart connection can be called upon for any workings with the Earth Mother energy, and the more it is called upon, the stronger it will become.

The following ceremony can be performed in nature, for a stronger connection, but can also be performed indoors, if privacy and secrecy is needed. No matter where you are, the heart to heart connection will take place.

You will need:

1 pink rose
4 clear quartz crystal points
1 rose quartz
1 white candle dressed with love oil and infused with love energy

Visualize a circle of green light surrounding you.

Place the rose, crystals, and candle on your altar, as diagramed:

```
        CANDLE              ROSE

              P
              O
              I
              N
              T

    POINT    ROSE QUARTZ    POINT

              P
              O
              I
              N
              T
```

The points should be facing away from the rose quartz, so the energy spreads out and around, within your green circle.

Light the candle and say:

> *"May this flame be my hearth,*
> *And connect to Mother Earth!*
> *Flame of heart burning bright,*
> *Connect now, through this light!"*

Stare into the flame as you feel the connection take place.

Once you feel connected, take the rose, and hold it up to your heart chakra, placing your projective (dominant) hand over it, and say:

**"Rose of pink,
May hearts link."**

With your receptive (non-dominant) hand, touch the rose quartz, as you say:

**"Earth connection,
From all directions!"**

Feel the connection strengthening, as the energy travels from the rose quarts, up through your receptive hand and arm, across your chest, down through your projective arm and hand, into the rose, and penetrating into your heart chakra. Focus on this current of energy for a few moments, as you stare into the flame of the white candle.

Place the rose on top of the rose quartz, and say:

**"Heart to Heart,
Connection start,
Earth Mother's love,
Around, below, and above;
Earth to heart,
May it never part!"**

Take a deep breath in, breathing in the power of the connection made, and exhaling all negative energy you may be carrying.

When the connection has reached the strength you are comfortable with, extinguish the candle as you say:

"Flame of light,
Now, take flight!
For thy connection,
And thy reflection,
I thank thee,
Blessed be!"

Place the rose in a safe place, as this is now the symbol of your heart to heart connection with the Earth Mother energy.

Note: Always practice fire safety!

Earth Mother Talisman

The Earth Mother energy can be used in a variety of ways. One of the ways is by that of a talisman of protection. This talisman can be used personally, in a car, or home, and offers protection channeled from the earth energy. It is very strong, and doesn't weaken over time.

To make the Earth Mother talisman, you will first need to create a connection to the Earth Mother energy, as talked about in this book.

Take a walk in nature, and locate two sticks that have already fallen from a tree. Never cut a branch to make this talisman! Cutting a branch suggests you have power over nature, and should never be done, especially when working magick with earth energy.

The two sticks should be about 4-6 inches in length, each. Crisscross the two sticks in the shape of an "X", and secure with a ribbon.

Next, place 3 heaping pinches of soil, a rock, and a fallen leaf, onto the center of a piece of material. Draw up the edges of the material, and tie off the bundle with a ribbon.

Secure the bundle to the sticks by a length of ribbon, and set the talisman out in the direct sunshine for 1-3 hours. Once this is complete, hold the talisman between your two palms and say:

"Earth Mother energy,
I now call unto thee-
May this talisman
Do all it can,
To protect,
And reflect;
Dissolving negativity,
Bringing peace and harmony!"

Carry the talisman with you for personal protection, place it in your car for travel protection, or place it in your home, above your front door, to protect your hearth and home. Keep the Earth Mother talisman on your altar or in a safe place when not using.

Smudging Ceremony

Smudging is a wonderful way to strip negative vibration away and replace it with a high vibration. This is generally done with sage, sweet grass, cedar, or palo santo.

You can make a smudge pot, which is a clay pot filled with soil. The incense or herbs are burned in it, and it usually sits upon an altar or in the center of a room, circle, or medicine wheel.

You can also use an abalone shell, which is held by hand, and the herbs are burned inside it, while a feather, or feather fan, is used to swirl the smoke up and over the person or area being smudged.

This ceremony is for smudging a sacred space, either in a medicine wheel, or a circle, usually, but can also be used in a room, or even throughout an entire home, to cleanse away negative energy.

Make sure you turn off all smoke alarms if this is performed indoors, and open all windows!

You will need:

Smudge pot or abalone shell
Feather or feather fan
Sage, cedar, sweet grass, or palo santo

In the center of your medicine wheel, circle, or room, light the herb in the pot or shell, and say:

> **"Sacred smoke,**
> **High vibration I invoke!**
> **Negativity clear away,**
> **Positive vibes come to stay!**
> **Earth Mother energy,**
> **Bring positive energy to me!**
> **By this smoke, I declare**
> **Cleansed space, smoke, and air!"**

Using the feather or fan, wave the smoke over the area, as you walk, spiraling out from the center, in a clockwise motion, until the entire area has been smudged. Once completed, say:

> **"May the Earth Mother bless,**
> **Cleanse, and consecrate this space!**
> **So mote it be!"**

You may place the remainder of the burning herb in the center of the sacred space until it completely burns itself out.

If you are sharing this smudging ritual with others, you may take turns smudging each other before the ceremony begins. If you are smudging solo, you may smudge yourself either before or after the ceremony, based upon your preference. Your energy will be smudged during the ceremony just by being in the sacred space.

Note: Always practice fire safety.

Earth Mother Magick

These magickal workings all need the Earth Mother energy, and in order to use them successfully, you will need to establish a working connection with the Earth Mother. The Earth Mother Meditation in this book will provide a starting point for building this connection easily.

To Make Earth Mother Oil

You will need:

Patchouli oil
Peppermint oil
Jasmine oil
Rosemary oil
Grapeseed oil
1oz amber bottle

In a 1oz. amber bottle, combine the following:

10 drops patchouli oil
7 drops jasmine oil

3 drops peppermint oil
3 drops rosemary oil

Swirl the bottle around to mix the oils, and add the grapeseed oil until bottle is mostly full. Swirl again, to blend the oils with the carrier oil, and bury it in the earth or in a pot of soil for 3 days, to charge with Earth Mother energy.

Store out of direct sunlight.

To Stop Interference

You will need:

Dragon's blood ink
Quill pen
Craft stick

Write the name of the person interfering in your affairs on the craft stick, using the ink and quill. Dig a hole in the ground they are sure to never find, and place the stick inside. As you bury the stick, say:

"Earth Mother, make this right,
Take this interference from my sight!
May (person's name) interfere no more,
As this stick becomes its' core.
Stop (person's name) in their tracks,
May their interference get the ax!
(Person's name), leave me be,
Earth Mother, thy assistance I ask of thee!"

When completely buried, stomp on the ground three times.

Earth Mother Guidance

You will need:

Pot of soil
Seed

As you plant the seed in the pot of soil, say:

> *"Gracious Mother Earth,*
> *Giver of life, home, and hearth;*
> *I ask thee, in my time of need;*
> *To guide me, help me plant this seed!*
> *As this growth takes place,*
> *So my choices, may I face.*
> *Grow, seed, grow!*
> *So I may reap what I sow,*
> *Earth Mother I ask of thee,*
> *Guide me now, Blessed be!"*

Water the seed, give it sunlight, and watch it grow, as the guidance you requested comes to you.

Earth Mother Prosperity Spell

You will need:

3 coins

Out in nature, dig three holes with the index finger of you projective (dominant) hand. Place one of the coins in the first hole, and bury it, as you say:

**"Coin one,
This spell has begun!"**

Place another coin in the second hole, and as you bury it, say:

**"Coin two,
Make it true!"**

Place the last coin in the last hole. As you bury it, say:

**"Coin three,
Bring prosperity to me!"**

Visualize money raining down on you, filling your needs of financial abundance.

Make sure the three coins are not disturbed until you have received the prosperity you have asked for. After retrieving the coins, place them in a safe place so you will never lose them.

Earth Strength Spell

Find a safe place to lay in nature. Take a deep breath, breathing in pure light, and exhaling all stress and negativity. Feel the earth energy absorb into you, as you say:

"Earth Mother, hear my call;
Lend thy strength, so I shan't fall,
I ask of thee, this, a boon,
By the powers of the Earth and moon!
Bring thy inner strength to me,
As I will it, so shall it be!"

To Find a Job

You will need:

Aventurine crystal
Green candle dressed with power and infused with Earth energy

On your altar, place the aventurine crystal in front of the green candle. Light the candle, and say:

"Earth Mother energy,
Bring to me
The job I seek
Within the week.
May I interview well,
By the power of this spell!

The perfect job for me,
So mote it be!"

Stare into the flame as you visualize getting the interview for your dream job, and being offered the position when the interview is complete.

Carry the aventurine crystal with you on the interview to add the power of the Earth Mother.

Note: Always practice fire safety.

To Bring Patience

You will need:

Clear quartz point

Surround yourself with white light. Hold the clear quartz point in your projective (dominant) hand and say:

"Mother of the Earth,
Life, death, rebirth-
A boon, I ask of thee,
I need patience shown to me!"

Look deeply into the clear quartz point, and ponder the length of time it took the Earth Mother to grow that specific crystal.

Take a deep breath, and accept that patience is necessary to manifest something so perfect and wonderful.

Carry the clear quartz point with you as a reminder, when you find yourself becoming impatient.

To Strengthen Divination Skills

You will need:

White candle

Light the white candle and say:

> *"Earth Mother, Divining light,*
> *Give to me, future sight!*
> *Show me the way,*
> *Every blessed day!*
> *Help me see,*
> *So mote it be!"*

Visualize your divination skills opening up and becoming very accurate. Be as detailed as possible during this visualization. Project the energy out that your divination skills are top notch, and you are in high demand for readings.

Note: Always practice fire safety.

Earth Incense

<u>You will need:</u>

Patchouli herb
Rosemary herb
Marjoram herb
Oak bark
Cinnamon spice
Dried rose petals
Mortar and pestle
Bowl

Using the mortar and pestle, grind all the ingredients, with the exception of the dried rose petals, into powder. Combine all the ingredients into the bowl, and with your projective (dominant) hand, mix them thoroughly. As you mix the ingredients, say:

> **"Earth with earth,**
> **Burn in hearth.**
> **Smoke will fume,**
> **Earth power resume!**
> **Flame ignite,**
> **Power with might!**
> **Incense for me,**
> **Blessed be!"**

Keep the incense stored in an airtight container, and use when working Earth Mother magick.

<u>Note: Always practice fire safety.</u>

You will need:

Green candle dressed with power oil and infused with earth energy

Surround yourself with golden light. Light the green candle, and say:

> **"Mother Earth,**
> **Find my worth,**
> **As flame burns fire,**
> **Manifest my desire!"**

Stare into the flame as you visualize all your desires coming to fruition.

Note: Always practice fire safety.

To Heal Back Pain

Sit with your back firmly against the trunk of a tree. Take a deep breath, inhaling earth energy, and exhaling pain. Say:

> **"Mighty tree,**
> **I ask of thee;**
> **Take my pain,**
> **May it wane,**
> **Away from me,**

So mote it be!"

Power Crystals

You will need:

3 crystals of any kind

Go out in nature, and find a secluded spot where you are least likely to be disturbed. Sit in silence, soaking up the earth energy surrounding you. Place the three crystals on the earth in front of you like this:

CRYSTAL   CRYSTAL   CRYSTAL

Feel your connection to the Earth Mother. Ask her to send her energy into the three crystals.

Visualize the three crystals soaking up the Earth Mother energy like they were a sponge soaking up water. When they are filled with the energy, give gratitude to the Earth Mother, collect the three crystals, and keep them in a safe place.

Use them when you are in need of a power boost for any magickal workings pertaining to the Earth Mother.

Earthy Potpourri

Airtight container
Orris root
Patchouli oil
Dried leaves
Twigs
Pine cones
Stones
Pods
Small bowl
Miscellaneous herbs

In the small bowl, place the orris root, and drop the patchouli oil directly on it, making sure you saturate each piece of orris root thoroughly.

In the airtight container, add all the remailing ingredients. Lastly, add the oil soaked orris root, and mix well, using your projective (dominant) hand.

Place in a decorative bowl to draw in Earth Mother energy.

When not in use, store in the airtight container. If scent dissipates, add more patchouli oil soaked orris root to the mixture.

To Bring Harmony

You will need:

Labradorite crystal

White candle dressed with blessing oil and infused with earth energy

Take a deep breath, breathing in Earth Mother energy, and exhaling stress and negativity. Light the white candle as you say:

"Earth Mother of things to be,
Bring now to me, harmony.
As in nature,
May my future
Focus on the balance,
Lined up at a glance,
And set it free,
Harmony for me!"

Hold the labradorite in your projective (dominant) hand as you stare into the flame and visualize every aspect of your life balanced in perfect harmony. Carry the labradorite with you to keep the harmonic energy of the Earth Mother with you at all times.

Note: Always practice fire safety.

Grounding Chaotic Energy

To ground chaotic energy, first shake all the energy into your hands. This might take some work. It may help to visualize purple light flowing in through your crown chakra, filling your body up, forcing the chaotic energy into your hands.

Once you feel all the energy accumulating in your hands, place them onto the earth, and connect to the Earth Mother energy.

This connection will naturally create a vacuum like action, where the chaotic energy will be automatically drawn out of your hands and absorbed into the earth.

When all the chaotic energy is gone, give gratitude to the Earth Mother for assisting.

<u>To Bring Beauty</u>

<u>You will need:</u>

A clear quartz crystal
Pink candle dressed with love oil and infused
with earth energy

Sit in nature, taking in all the natural beauty surrounding you. Breathe in the earth energies all around you.

Visualize a pink light surrounding you. Light the pink candle as you say:

"Beauty find me,
Show the way,
Help me to see,
Night and day,
Come to me now,
Show me how,

Bring me beauty,
So mote it be!"

Sit in silence, feeling nature's beauty all around you, being absorbed into you.

Carry the clear quartz with you to remind you that you are part of the beauty of nature, which is perfect and balanced at all times.

Note: Always practice fire safety.

To Heal Illness

Find a quiet place in nature where you will least likely be disturbed. Lay down onto the earth. Relax your entire body.

Take a deep breath, breathing in the Earth Mother energy that surrounds you. As you exhale, blow out the illness that you want to heal.

Feel the magnetic force of the earth energy draw the illness out of your relaxed body, and absorb it into the soil beneath you.

Lay for as long as needed, until you feel all the illness leave your body. When ready, rise up, and thank the Earth Mother for the healing you have just received.

For Personal Growth

You will need:

Pot of soil
Seeds
Clear quartz crystal

Visualize a golden light surrounding you. Hold the seeds in your projective (dominant) hand, and say:

> **"Earth Mother energy,**
> **Bring personal growth to me;**
> **I now inspire**
> **To grow even higher,**
> **Becoming a better me,**
> **As I will it, so shall it be!"**

Place the clear quartz crystal on top of the soil, in the center of the pot. Plant the seeds in the pot of soil, around the clear quartz crystal.

Be sure to water the seeds and give them adequate sunshine. As the seeds grow, so will you.

Self-Love Spell

You will need:

Pink candle dressed with love oil and infused

with earth energy

Sit in nature, allowing the Earth Mother energy fill you. Feel the pulsing of the energy match your heartbeat. Understand that you are part of the miracle of nature. Light the pink candle and say:

"Earth Mother energy,
Around, below, and above;
I am in need, bring to me
A powerful dose of self-love.
I know I am a part of you,
I just need to connect
To all you are, say, and do;
So I can resurrect
And make my heart whole
By self-loving me
Body, mind, and soul
Bless me, blessed be!"

Stare into the flame as you visualize the earth energy filling you with self-love. This should be done until you feel the love vibration fill you.

Note: Always practice fire safety.

For Motivation

Sit in nature, with your back against the trunk of a tree, and connect to the Earth Mother energy. Allow this energy to fill you, energizing you, until you are motivated. Give thanks for the energy.

Charging Crystals with Earth Mother Energy

Using Earth Mother energy to charge crystals is a wonderful way to keep the vibration of a crystal high. This is especially useful for crystals that are used frequently, for healing or magick.

When using a crystal, the energy of the stone gets dirty and drained. Cleaning and charging these crystals keep them in high vibration, so they are always ready to work with when needed.

There are a couple ways to charge a crystal with earth energy. The easiest, is to cleanse the crystal and bury it into the earth. Always mark where the crystal was buried, so you do not lose it!

You can also bury it in a pot of soil. This is handy if you do not have easy access to the earth. An example would be someone who lives in a city high rise apartment.

The other way is to cleanse the crystal, then hold it in your projective (dominant) hand while you use the Earth Mother Meditation in this book. While you are in the cave with the crystal energy, channel that energy into your crystal.

It's as easy as that!

During the meditation, you can also ask the Earth Mother to send power to your crystal.

Usually, she will do this naturally, because of the earth energy connection she shares with the crystal already.

Reading Signs in Nature

While walking through nature, clear your mind of all mundane thoughts, ground and center your energy, and listen to the silence around you. Listen to the breeze blowing; hear the rustling of the leaves around you.

Nature will give you messages if you open yourself up to receive them.

Watch the leaves. Do you see one leaf moving differently than the others? It may be a dryad spirit saying "hi".

Feel the vibration all around you. Can you feel the shift in energy as you move through the trees? Maybe a specific tree calls to you stronger than the others, or something unusual calls to your attention for reasons unknown.

By listening to what we see, hear, and feel, we can learn to communicate with the spirits of nature. Once we develop this ability, we can read the signs and messages of nature to predict changes in the weather and our environment, and even bond with the forces of nature.

Tree Spirits

Connecting to and working with tree spirits is a very rewarding form of Earth Mother magick. The act of making the effort to connect, in itself, will bring the earth energy to you.

One of the most popular ways of connection is to find a tree, approach it with love in your heart, and gently hug it, sharing that love vibration with the tree. At this time, you can also send the tree healing, talk to it, or just share breath with it. Allow your heartbeat to pulse with the energy of the tree.

Another easy way to connect is to sit up with your back against the trunk of the tree, and allow your energies to intertwine. This exchange of energy can be used to heal both, you and the tree at the same time.

Whenever you receive a healing from the tree spirits, always remember to leave an offering of thanks. This can be done by singing the tree spirits a song, leaving a crystal or other trinket charged with your gratitude, or offering a meal.

Shamanic Journeying is another successful way to communicate with the tree spirits. This method builds a strong rapport with the nature spirits. If you are already familiar with journeying, I highly suggest using this method.

If you are not familiar, and wish to learn, my suggestion would be to find a teacher, or shamanic healing circle to work with you, or start with a shamanic journey book.

Once you are able to establish a working relationship with the tree spirits, your connection to the Earth Mother will intensify, and your earth magick will gain power.

Honoring the 7 Directions and Associated Beings

There is more to working with earth energies than the Earth Mother and nature spirits. There are the 7 directions, which are North, South, East, West, Center, Above, and Below.

With these directions are the beings that are associated with them. Each direction has a being, or spirit, that you can connect to, just like connecting to tree spirits or to the Earth Mother.

This connection is made either through shamanic journey or meditation. When you are working with a specific direction, having a good rapport with the spirit being that is associated will increase the power of the magickal working.

When working with these spirit beings, it is very important to honor them with recognition and gratitude.

This can be done with song, prayer, or chanting. An offering can also be made, but is not as common as giving recognition and thanks.

Medicine Wheel

The medicine wheel is a very sacred way to draw power from the Earth Mother. This version of using a medicine wheel is not traditional, but still very effective.

To set up a personal medicine wheel, you will first need to purify the ground and declare it sacred space. This can be done by sweeping and cleansing the energy of the space you want to use. To sweep the energy, using a besom, sweep the energy from east to west, making sure every spot of the space is swept. Next, using a spray bottle, mix sea salt and spring water, and mist the entire area. Finally, smudge the space and declare it sacred.

Now that your sacred space is purified, the next step is to shield it from unwanted energy. For this, you will need to charge 8 large crystal points with protection and reflection. Place a crystal point at each of the four directions, and then at every combined direction. There should be a crystal point at the following directions:

N, NE, E, SE, S, SW, W, NW

Make sure the points are facing outward from the sacred space, so any unwanted energy will be reflected away from your medicine wheel.

Now that your sacred space is protected, it is time to set up the medicine wheel. To do this, you will need 5 large stones, and 12 smaller stones. These stones need to be big enough that you will easily see them. The small stones should be no smaller than a softball, and the large stones should be no bigger than a basketball.

Start by placing 4 of the large stones in the four cardinal directions:

N, S, E, W

Place the last large stone directly in the center. Now you can use the 12 small stones to connect the large stones in a circle by placing 3 small stones between each of the cardinal directions.

Once this is done, your medicine wheel is set up! Next you will need to activate it. Walk the perimeter of the circle as you sprinkle a mixture of cornmeal, seeds, and sage. Walk the circle several times; sprinkling this mixture so there is a solid circle of the mixture surrounding the medicine wheel.

Next, you will want to use a shamanic drum or rattle, to call in the ancestors, spirit helpers, Earth Mother, and any other guardians you wish to bring into your medicine wheel.

Use your medicine wheel to raise medicine power for healing or magick. You can also use your medicine wheel as your sacred space to use any of the ceremonies or magickal workings found in this book. This wheel is your sacred space.

When you have completed your magickal workings, you can release your wheel by giving a gift of gratitude to all the helping spirits and declaring your wheel released.

Raise Medicine Power

Once your medicine wheel is set and activated, raising medicine power is accomplished by praying, dancing, singing, or any other act of giving energy to start the medicine working to grow in power. The energy is started and built up until it reaches its peak of power.

The most commonly used method of raising medicine power is to start with a prayer, then dance the prayer from the heart until the energy peaks. Sometimes a song comes naturally, and should be sung with intent.

Once the peak of power is reached, the medicine power is absorbed in for healing, or released to receive a magickal boost to an Earth Mother energy working.

Once the energy is absorbed or released, gratitude should always be given, along with an offering of thanks to the helping spirits and to the Earth Mother.

Giving Thanks to the Earth Mother

Whenever you work with the Earth Mother energy, it is vital that gratitude is always given. This gift of gratitude replenishes the Earth Mother and the energy we use during our workings with her.

Gratitude to the Earth Mother is given with prayer, chanting, offerings of gifts or food, and earth healing work. A prayer ribbon is a beautiful and thoughtful way to show gratitude. It also serves as a reminder of the Earth Mother connection we have established.

To make a prayer ribbon, find a ribbon that is at least 3 feet long or longer. Longer is always better if you are going to be doing a lot of Earth energy work. Choose a tree that you will be working with, and ask the tree permission to tie the ribbon to one of its branches. Once permission is given, gently tie your ribbon to a sturdy branch.

As you work with the Earth Mother and nature energies, you can make little medicine bundles and tie them to the ribbon as offerings of gratitude.

A medicine bundle is easy to make, and shows strong gratitude to the Earth Mother. To make a medicine bundle, you will need a piece of cloth, an offering of either sage, sweet grass, tobacco, or cedar, a piece of your hair or fingernail clipping, a stone, shell, or feather, and a small ribbon to tie the bundle up with.

Place all the contents in the center of the cloth, and pull up all sides, then secure it closed with the ribbon. Once the bundle is complete, hold it between your palms and say a prayer of thanks.

Your prayer can be very detailed to the reason you are thankful. All that is left to do is to tie the medicine bundle to the ribbon tied to the tree.

You can tie other gifts to the ribbon as well, and add more ribbons as needed. Just always ask permission to tie the ribbon, and remember, once an offering is tied to the ribbon, it is no longer yours, and should not be removed.

If the ribbon breaks or is blown off by wind, you may collect the ribbon and put it is a safe place to keep for the Earth Mother.

If the ribbon is removed by another, do not fret, as the Earth Mother will still receive your gifts of gratitude, and will understand the situation.

When choosing ribbon color, always go with what feels right with the connection of the Earth Mother energy based on the work being done.

Medicine Bundle Blessing

Sometimes, the magickal workings with the Earth Mother energy are spread out over a period of time, and although each session receives gratitude, a detailed prayer for a medicine bundle becomes repetitive. In this instance, you can use a basic medicine bundle blessing like this one:

"With gratitude and love,
Below, around, and above;
I offer this bundle to thee,
Earth Mother energy;
To show appreciation to thee,
For magick thou has given freely!
May this medicine bundle be,
A gift of thanks for you from me!"

Elemental Blessing Ceremony

When working with the Earth Mother energy for any magickal need, you can strengthen the energy being used by adding the elemental energy to it.

This elemental blessing ceremony is set up to bless a piece of magickal jewelry, but can be easily adapted to bless any magickal tool, talisman, stone, or medicine bundle.

It is up to you, on what you choose to bless with the elemental energy.

You will need:

1 white candle
1 red candle
1 bowl of salt
1 bowl of spring water
Incense or smudging herbs
1 piece of magickal jewelry

Place the white candle in the center of your circle or medicine wheel. Place the red candle in the south, the bowl of water in the west, the bowl of salt in the north, and the incense in the east.

Visualize a circle of white light surrounding you.

Start in the east. Pass the jewelry through the incense smoke as you say:

"With this smoke,
I bless this (jewelry)
With the element of air.
May this blessing bring me
Communication and creativity.
Blessed be!"

Move to the south. Pass the jewelry through the flame of the red candle as you say:

"With this flame,
I bless this (jewelry)
With the element of fire.
May this blessing bring me
Passion and courage.
Blessed be!"

Move to the west. Dip the jewelry into the bowl of spring water as you say:

"With this water,
I bless this (jewelry)
With the element of water.
May this blessing bring me
Movement and intuition.
Blessed be!"

Move to the north. Sprinkle the jewelry with the salt as you say:

"With this salt,
I bless this (jewelry)
With the element of earth.
May this blessing bring me
Stability and strength.
Blessed be!"

Move to the center. Suspend the jewelry over the flame of the white candle as you say:

"Spirit of Akasha,
Bless this (Jewelry)
With thy essence.
May it bring me
Blessings in abundance.
Blessed be!"

Wear the jewelry for 24 hours, as you open yourself up to receive the blessings being given. As you recognize a blessing coming to fruition, be sure to give a prayer of thanks to the element that gifted you the blessing.

Make sure you keep the jewelry on your altar or in a safe place when you are not wearing it.

Note: Always practice fire safety.

Earth Mother Blessing

To bless an item or magickal tool with the Earth Mother energy, you will need to be out in nature, or if this is not possible, you may use a pot of soil.

If you have already built a connection with the Earth Mother, you will want to call upon her for this blessing. If you have not, it is recommended that you use the meditation in this book to have an initial connection before using this blessing.

This ceremony may take place indoors if need be, but is preferred to be held out in nature.

You will need:

Item to be blessed
Pot of soil if nature is unavailable

Sit for a moment and ground your energy. Visualize a circle of green light surrounding you. Call upon your connection to the Earth Mother. Once the connection is made, take a moment to fill yourself with the Earth Mother energy.

Hold the item to be blessed over your heart chakra with your projective (dominant) hand while you place your receptive (non-dominant) hand on the earth, or in the pot of soil, so you have a direct earth energy connection.

Feel the vibration from the earth flow up through your receptive side and out through your projective side, flowing into the item to be blessed.

Feel the energy as you fill the item with this flow of earth vibration. Once you feel the item pulsating with this energy, take a deep breath and say:

"Mother Earth,
Home and hearth,
I ask thee
To bless this (item) for me,
So I may
Connect to you every day,
And access your power

Every hour.
By the magick of thee,
Blessed be!"

Once the blessing is complete, keep the item on your altar or in a safe place when not in use.

Earth Mother Healing Ceremony

This ceremony is to assist the Earth Mother in healing, and can be held as often as needed. Unlike the other ceremonies in this book, this ceremony needs to be held outside, in nature.

It is intended for an individual to perform, but can easily be adapted to include a group of practitioners.

This ceremony calls for use of a few shamanic tools. The shamanic tube can be made from clay, bone, wood, or even paper. The rattle can be substituted with a closed container and a handful of seeds or pebbles, and the drum can be substituted with a kitchen pot, or other similar item. Feel free to be creative!

You will need:

Shamanic rattle

Shamanic drum
Shamanic tube

Within a medicine wheel or circle upon sacred space, visualize a circle of golden light surrounding the entire area. Directly within the ring of golden light, visualize a second light of green, filling the space within the circle.

Take a moment to connect with the Earth Mother energy. This may be accomplished by song, chant, or prayer, unless a working relationship is already established through previous workings.

Once the connection is in place, take a deep breath, and as you exhale, say:

> ***"I breathe out the fire of pain!"***

Take another deep breath, and as you exhale, say:

> ***"I breathe out the flame of destruction!"***

Take a third deep breath, and upon exhale, say:

> ***"I breathe out the smoke of damage!"***

Place your projective (dominant) hand over your heart chakra, and your receptive (non-dominant) hand onto the earth. Feel the energy of the Earth Mother pulsate up through your receptive hand and arm, across your chest, and down through your projective arm and hand.

Feel the energy, pay close attention to where the healing is needed, and to what is causing the ailment to take place. Once you understand the cause of the pain, and where the healing is needed, switch your hands, so your projective hand is now on the earth, and your receptive hand is on your hearth chakra.

Feel the flow of energy reverse, sending your love and compassion down into the Earth Mother.

Using the shamanic tube, take a deep breath of healing energy and blow it onto the earth, through the tube. Be sure to leave about an inch or two between the tube and the ground. Keep repeating this process, moving freely around inside the circle of light, until you have blown the healing energy surrounding you, into all the areas of the medicine wheel.

Once complete, Seal the energy with the shamanic rattle, by rattling over the entire area of the medicine wheel.

When the entire area has been sealed, Lay a layer of protection over the circle, using the shamanic drum.

This beat should be loud, fast, and steady.

Upon completion, give gratitude to the Earth Mother, send her well wishes, and pray for her healing to encompass her entire being. Visualize the golden and green light expanding, and covering the entire planet with healing energy.

Earth Chanting

Earth chanting is a wonderful way to draw upon and share Earth Mother energy. It is most successful while sitting in nature, usually done before the Earth Mother meditation or any magickal working or medicine wheel ceremony.

In nature, find a comfortable spot where you will not be easily disturbed. Take a few deep breaths, breathing in the earth energy around you, and exhaling pent up stress and negativity.

Once relaxed, feel your connection to the Earth Mother, and start chanting!

Each chant is repeated until the desired energy flow is achieved. This usually happens in 3-5 repeats. These chants can be used repetitively, if raising a cone of power is your goal, and can even be sung when dancing a medicine wheel circle.

Feel free to write your own chants as well! Let it come from the heart while you are connected!

Earth Rebirth

"Earth, earth!
Heal thee,
Earth, earth!
Rebirth!"

Earth Is Changing

"Earth is changing,
Earth is changing!
Let change come!
Let change come!
Bring her healing,
Bring her healing!
The time has come!
The time has come!"

The Earth Is Home

"The earth is home
To so many,
The earth is home
To so many!
We must love our home,
We must heal our home!
The earth is home
To so many,
We must save her!"

Mother Earth I Hear You

"Mother Earth, I hear you;
Mother Earth, I hear you.
Your heart beats with mine,
Your heart beats with mine!
We are one within the circle,
We are one within the circle.
Part of the Divine,
Part of the Divine!"

Beauty Surrounds

"Beauty surrounds,
The trees and grounds.
Beauty surrounds,
The trees and grounds.
Take in her beauty,
Take in her beauty,
Let it surround your heart,
Let it surround your heart!"

Let it Rain

"Let it rain,
Let it rain!
Let it saturate the earth,
Let it rain,
Let it rain,
Let it give nature's rebirth!"

Closing Prayer

May the collective energy
Of love and compassion
Circle around the Earth Mother,
And heal her.
May the love and compassion
within us,
Assist in the process,
And bring in a new tomorrow for the future.
With love for the Earth Mother,
Blessed be!

100 Days Of Gratitude To Magically Transform The Soul

Ella C Moon

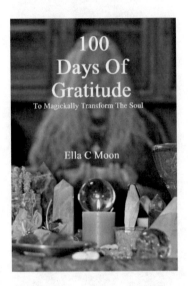

So often, we find ourselves wrapped up in our daily lives, dealing with all sorts of emotional ups and downs. Daily balancing of our energy, our chakras, and our mind-body-spirit connection becomes difficult, or even impossible.

This causes a disconnect between our physical and spiritual lives, which in turn, causes a disconnect within humanity and the elemental world surrounding us. Once the disconnect takes place, the love vibration within us stops expanding beyond our personal space and extending to others around us.

If you can rearrange your daily routine to include 30 minutes to re-establish the mind-body-spirit connection, you can transform yourself into a high love vibration being, which is what we all strive to do on a spiritual level.

A Book Of
Lights And Shadows
For The Seasoned Witch

Ella C Moon

Looking for a true Book of Shadows? You have found it! *A Book Of Lights And Shadows For The Seasoned Witch* is full of spells, recipes, rituals, prayers, and everything a witch will need for a magickal life.

There are no beginner directions in this book! This book is for the experienced witch.

Becoming The Witch

Ella C Moon

Raising vibration and balancing Ego are always a great goal for every witch. Want to know how? *Becoming The Witch* is a perfect place to start!

Becoming The Witch offers an in-depth look to truly understanding the Self, and finding the inner balance that is needed to evolve ourselves on a spiritual level.

Bohemian Magick

Ella C Moon

Bohemian Magick: For the Boho Spirited Witch is a must have in your magickal library! Indie Author Ella C Moon takes you on a step by step journey to freeing your wild heart and embracing your inner gypsy while inspiring others to greatness with unique ceremonies, fun crystal grids, enchanting recipes, and so much more! *Bohemian Magick* is an uplifting magickal book for the boho witch in all of us!

Make Magick Happen!

By The Light Of The Crystal Moon

Ella C Moon

Tired of the general portrayal of a witch being a negative figure? Me too! It is time for witches to be seen as the brilliant shining powers that we are! Shine in beauty!

By The Light Of The Crystal Moon is a book of Pagan poetry and short stories written to inspire and entertain.

Crystal Skull Magick

Ella C Moon

What is it about a crystal skull that provokes such fascination? Is it the sheer mystery of their origin and purpose? Is it their magnificent beauty? Or is it something else?

The power of the Crystal Skulls can be easily tapped into and used magickally. In *Crystal Skull Magick*, you will discover many ways to connect to the crystal skull power and use it for healing, divination, and several other magickal ways.

Divine Influences

Ella C Moon

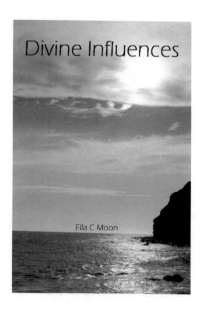

Divine Influences is a divination system channeled from Divinity through a meditation.

By using *Divine Influences*, you will see a big difference in your daily life. You will notice great things coming into your life and happening around you because when you are guided by Divinity, your personal vibration is raised, which attracts wonderful things to you!

Earth Mother Magick

Ella C Moon

Do you feel connected to the Earth energies? Or are you looking to increase that connection? This is the book for you! *Earth Mother Magick* shares spells and rituals that will assist you in connecting to the Earth on a deeper spiritual level, not just on an elemental one.

Earth Mother Magick includes Medicine Wheel Ceremony, Smudging Ceremony, Prayer Bundles, and so much more!

Magickal Enlightenment

Ella C Moon

New to the craft? Looking for a book that will guide you along your way? Magickal Enlightenment is an easy reference of basic magick for those beginning their journey. Understanding how magick works is the key to successful magickal workings. In this book, the basics of magick are broken down into an easily understood and followed format. Including spells, chants, and other easy to use magickal workings, Magickal Enlightenment is the perfect book to explain magickal workings and how to use them effectively.

Magickal Journal

Ella C Moon

Keeping records on your magickal journey is an amazing way to remember prominent occurrences, track your progress and most of all, see your results. *Magickal Journal* is designed to help you do just that! Internationally published Author, Ella C Moon, has created an easy to use format for tracking dreams, meditations, spellwork, and so much more! *Magickal Journal* also includes several pages of useful at-a-glance charts to guide you with quick references, to assist you in streamlining your focus and energy to your magickal intentions. With well over 325 pages, *Magickal Journal* will hold all of your spiritual records and results easily at your fingertips!

Seasonal Magick

Ella C Moon

Seasonal Magick is go-to for all your magickal needs. Spells, rituals, and recipes for every turn of the wheel can be found within these pages.

Seasonal Magick is a perfect spellbook for the beginner or adept witch, with all you need to celebrate the seasonal changes of Nature at your fingertips.

The Pagan Clergy Book Of Rituals And Ceremonies

Ella C Moon

The Pagan Clergy Book Of Rituals And Ceremonies has been created specifically for Pagan Clergy. It is in no way a beginner book. The rituals and ceremonies within these pages are intended to be used by trained and experienced, initiated Pagan Clergy only.

Thrifty Witch

Ella C Moon

Witchcraft on a Budget!

Who said you have to be rich to be a witch? There are so many resources for witches on a budget, and this book will reveal them all to you!

Packed with spells, rituals, recipes, and crystal grids, *Thrifty Witch* will give you just what you need!

Witch Box
How To Make And Use A Portable Altar Box

Ella C Moon

A Witch's Box is a traveling altar for the witch on the go. It consists of a box that holds a small version of main altar tools and spell supplies, so every witch will have those items available no matter where they are.

When the need arises, a witch can pull out their Witch Box, and take care of a house blessing or cleansing, a healing spell, or even a full moon ritual on the fly!

A Witch's Box is a must for any witch that travels or is for hire to perform various magickal duties.

The Power Of I AM
"I AM" Chanting for Positive Change

Ella C Moon

Change is necessary for growth. The hardest thing about change is determining what changes need to be made for our best and highest good. Once we figure out the changes that need to take place, the actual changing is easy to do.

The physical body and the etheric (energy) body need to be exact to exist in the same time and space. Any changes we make to our energy body will cause the physical body to shift and match it. By using the I AM chanting to shift our etheric body, it will also shift our physical body and all things in our physical world.

The technique of I AM chanting is efficient, easy, and fun to use.

Voodoo Doll Diary

Ella C Moon

A voodoo doll is a representation of a person, without having the actual person present. In the healing system of Reiki, as well as many other healing modalities, a remote healing is given through the use of a surrogate. This surrogate is usually either another person, a doll, or a stuffed animal. We can also use a drawing or photo as a surrogate. That is what this book is providing for us. A diary of surrogate healing through the use of a diagramed "voodoo doll".

Made in the USA
Columbia, SC
02 December 2023